Paleo Air Fryer Cookbook 2023

Satisfy Your Cravings with 40 Nutrient-Rich, Delicious & Healthy Paleo Air-Fryer Recipes

By

Dr. John A. Roberts

Copyright © 2023 John Roberts

All rights reserved. No part of this publication may be reproduced, distributed, or transmitted in any form or by any means, including photocopying, recording, or other electronic or mechanical methods, without the prior written permission of the publisher, except in the case of brief quotations embodied in critical reviews and certain other noncommercial uses permitted by copyright law.

Table of Contents

INTRODUCTION..**7**
CHAPTER ONE..**13**
  Getting Started with Your Air Fryer........................13
CHAPTER TWO..**19**
  Paleo Pantry Staples and Ingredients: Foods to Eat, Avoid, and Eat in Moderation..................................19
    Foods to Eat..19
    Foods to Avoid..21
    Foods to Eat in Moderation............................22
CHAPTER THREE..**25**
  Breakfast Delights: Energizing Paleo Air Fryer Recipes..25
    Crispy Bacon and Egg Cups:..........................25
    Sweet Potato Hash Browns............................26
    Veggie Omelette...27
    Banana Walnut Muffins..................................28
    Cinnamon Apple Chips...................................30
CHAPTER FOUR..**31**
  Appetizers and Snacks: Crispy Bites of Paleo Perfection...31
    Crispy Sweet Potato Fries..............................31
    Crispy Chicken Wings....................................32
    Zucchini Fritters...33
    Stuffed Mushrooms..34
    Coconut Shrimp...36
CHAPTER FIVE..**39**
  Wholesome Chicken and Poultry Dishes: A Flavorful Twist..39
    Crispy Air Fryer Chicken Tenders...................39
    Lemon Herb Air Fryer Chicken Breast...........40
    Buffalo Air Fryer Wings..................................42

    Herb-Roasted Air Fryer Turkey Breast...............43
    Moroccan Spiced Air Fryer Cornish Hens..........44
CHAPTER SIX...**47**
  Succulent Seafood: Oceanic Delights Made Paleo. 47
    Crispy Air Fryer Coconut Shrimp.......................47
    Lemon Garlic Air Fryer Salmon.........................48
    Cajun Air Fryer Shrimp Skewers.......................49
    Garlic Butter Air Fryer Scallops.........................51
    Lemon Herb Air Fryer Halibut...........................52
CHAPTER SEVEN..**55**
  Tender and Juicy Beef, Pork, and Lamb Recipes...55
    Air Fryer Steak Bites...55
    Crispy Air Fryer Pork Chops..............................56
    Garlic Herb Air Fryer Lamb Chops....................57
    Spicy Air Fryer Meatballs...................................59
    Smoky Air Fryer Ribs...60
CHAPTER EIGHT...**63**
  Flavorful Vegetable Creations: A Plant-Powered Feast..63
    Crispy Air Fryer Brussels Sprouts......................63
    Parmesan Air Fryer Asparagus..........................64
    Spicy Air Fryer Cauliflower Bites......................65
    Herb-Roasted Air Fryer Carrots.........................66
    Crispy Air Fryer Zucchini Fries.........................67
CHAPTER NINE...**69**
  Side Dishes and Sauces: Perfect Complements to Any Meal...69
    Garlic Rosemary Air Fryer Sweet Potato Wedges
....69
    Crispy Air Fryer Onion Rings............................70
    Lemon Garlic Air Fryer Broccoli.......................71
    Creamy Avocado Dip...72
    Tangy Balsamic Glaze..73
CHAPTER TEN...**75**

Irresistible Paleo Air Fryer Desserts: Satisfy Your
Sweet Tooth..75
    Coconut Flour Chocolate Chip Cookies..............75
    Apple Crisp..76
    Paleo Donuts...78
    Cinnamon-Spiced Sweet Potato Fries................80
    Coconut Shrimp...81
CHAPTER ELEVEN..**83**
    Tips and Tricks for Perfect Paleo Air Frying............83
CONCLUSION...**89**

INTRODUCTION

Emily, a vibrant and ambitious woman, found herself at a crossroads when her health took a sudden turn. Battling a chronic illness, she knew it was time to prioritize her well-being. Inspired by stories of others who had found healing through nutrition, Emily embarked on a journey to embrace a paleo lifestyle.

Equipped with an air fryer, a versatile kitchen companion, Emily began her exploration of delicious and nutrient-rich paleo recipes. She discovered a world of culinary possibilities that would nourish her body and delight her taste buds.

With each recipe she tried, Emily experienced the transformative power of healthy eating. The air fryer allowed her to recreate her favorite dishes without sacrificing flavor or nutrition. Crispy chicken wings, perfectly roasted vegetables, and mouthwatering salmon fillets became staples in her kitchen.

As she embraced the paleo diet, Emily noticed remarkable changes in her health. Her energy levels soared, and she felt a renewed sense of vitality. The nutrient-dense meals she prepared not only supported her physical well-being but also provided a sense of comfort and satisfaction.

Emily's culinary adventures in the kitchen became her therapy, a creative outlet that filled her days with joy. She experimented with new ingredients, spices, and flavors, constantly expanding her repertoire of paleo air fryer recipes.

Word of Emily's journey spread, and friends and family marveled at her newfound vitality. They were inspired to join her in the pursuit of healthier living. Emily's kitchen became a gathering place where loved ones could savor the goodness of nutritious meals prepared with love.

Through her determination and culinary exploration, Emily not only healed her own body but also touched the lives of those around her. Her story of resilience and the transformative power of food became an inspiration for others seeking a path to wellness.

In the end, Emily's journey taught her that embracing a healthy lifestyle isn't just about the food we eat, but about the love and care we put into nourishing ourselves. The paleo diet and the air fryer became her allies in this pursuit, forever changing her life and the lives of those she touched.

The paleo diet has gained significant popularity in recent years due to its numerous health benefits. This ancestral eating approach focuses on consuming whole, unprocessed foods that our ancestors would have eaten during the Paleolithic era. By eliminating grains, dairy, and processed foods, the paleo diet encourages a return to nutrient-dense foods that support optimal health.

Studies have shown that the paleo diet can lead to several positive outcomes. Research indicates that following a paleo diet can improve markers of cardiovascular health, such as reducing blood pressure and cholesterol levels. It has also been associated with weight loss and improved insulin sensitivity, making it an effective approach for managing diabetes and metabolic syndrome.

The combination of the paleo diet with the usage of air fryers has further enhanced the health benefits of this eating approach. Air fryers use hot air circulation to cook food, reducing the need for excessive oil. This results in lower fat content in meals, making them healthier and more heart-friendly. Air frying also helps to retain the natural flavors and textures of the ingredients, creating delicious and crispy dishes without compromising on taste.

Statistics in the United States highlight the growing popularity of both the paleo diet and air fryer usage. According to a survey conducted by the National Health and Nutrition Examination Survey (NHANES), approximately 3% of adults in the United States follow a paleo or similar low-carbohydrate diet. This number has been steadily increasing as more individuals recognize the benefits of this eating approach.

Similarly, the use of air fryers has seen a significant rise in recent years. According to market research, the global air fryer market is expected to reach a value of over $1 billion by 2026, with the United States being one of the key regions driving this growth. The convenience, health benefits, and versatility of air fryers have made them a popular choice for health-conscious individuals looking to prepare delicious meals with less oil.

The combination of the paleo diet and air fryer usage offers a powerful and effective way to support overall health and wellness. By embracing nutrient-dense, whole foods and utilizing the innovative cooking capabilities of air fryers, individuals can enjoy the benefits of a healthy diet while savoring delicious meals. Whether it's reducing the risk of chronic diseases or simply enjoying flavorful and satisfying dishes, the paleo diet and air fryer usage provide a winning combination for a healthier lifestyle.

CHAPTER ONE

Getting Started with Your Air Fryer

Air fryers have become incredibly popular in recent years, thanks to their ability to create delicious, crispy meals with significantly less oil than traditional frying methods. If you've recently acquired an air fryer and are eager to start cooking up some tasty dishes, this guide will walk you through the essential steps to get started with your new kitchen gadget.

Read the Instruction Manual: Before using your air fryer, take the time to read the instruction manual thoroughly. Familiarize yourself with the different parts, functions, and safety precautions specific to your model. Understanding how to properly operate your air fryer will ensure optimal performance and prevent any accidents or damage.

Preheat the Air Fryer: **Just like preheating an oven, preheating your air fryer is crucial for achieving the best cooking results. Set the desired temperature and allow the air fryer to preheat for a few minutes before placing your food inside. Preheating helps to create a hot and evenly distributed cooking environment, ensuring that your food cooks thoroughly and becomes crispy.**

Start with Simple Recipes: **As a beginner, it's best to start with simple recipes that require minimal preparation and cooking time. Try making air-fried french fries, chicken wings, or vegetable skewers to get familiar with the cooking process. These recipes typically require basic ingredients and provide a good foundation for understanding how your air fryer works.**

Adjust Cooking Times and Temperatures: **Cooking times and temperatures may vary depending on the size, brand, and model of your air fryer. It's important to keep an eye on your food as it cooks and make adjustments accordingly. Start with the recommended cooking times provided in** recipes and monitor your food for doneness. You may need to adjust the temperature or cooking time slightly to achieve your desired results.

Use Parchment Paper or Cooking Spray: To prevent food from sticking to the air fryer basket, you can line it with parchment paper or use a light coating of cooking spray. This will make cleanup easier and ensure that your food releases effortlessly from the basket. However, be mindful of the cooking spray you choose, as some may cause excessive smoke or unpleasant odors when heated at high temperatures.

Experiment with Seasonings and Marinades: One of the great advantages of using an air fryer is the ability to infuse your food with flavors using various seasonings and marinades. Experiment with different combinations of herbs, spices, and sauces to add depth and complexity to your dishes. The hot circulating air in the fryer helps to intensify the flavors, resulting in mouthwatering meals.

Don't Overcrowd the Basket: It's essential to avoid overcrowding the air fryer basket. When food is overcrowded, it can prevent proper air circulation, leading to uneven cooking. Allow enough space between the food items to ensure they cook evenly and become crispy. If you have a large quantity of food to cook, it's better to cook them in batches.

Flip or Shake the Food: For even cooking, it's a good practice to flip or shake the food halfway through the cooking process. This helps to ensure that all sides of the food are exposed to the hot air, resulting in evenly cooked and crispy results. Use tongs or a spatula to gently flip or shake the food without damaging the coating or breading.

Keep an Eye on Cooking Progress: Unlike traditional frying methods, where you can easily observe the cooking progress, an air fryer's closed basket may make it a bit challenging to check on your food. However, it's important to keep an eye on the cooking progress to avoid overcooking or burning. Use the transparent window or open the basket briefly to check the doneness of your food.

Clean and Maintain Your Air Fryer: Proper cleaning and maintenance will ensure that your air fryer stays in excellent condition and continues to provide great cooking results. Always allow the air fryer to cool down completely before cleaning. Clean the basket and accessories with warm, soapy water or place them in the dishwasher if they are dishwasher safe. The exterior of the air fryer should be wiped with a damp cloth. Regularly check and clean the heating element and air vents to remove any accumulated food particles.

By following these tips and guidelines, you'll be well on your way to mastering your air fryer and creating delicious meals with ease. Enjoy the benefits of healthier, crispy cooking without compromising on taste and indulge in a wide variety of recipes that your air fryer can effortlessly handle. So, get ready to explore the culinary possibilities and embark on a flavorful journey with your air fryer!

CHAPTER TWO

Paleo Pantry Staples and Ingredients: Foods to Eat, Avoid, and Eat in Moderation

The Paleo diet, also known as the Paleolithic or Caveman diet, is based on the concept of eating foods that our ancestors consumed during the Paleolithic era. The diet focuses on whole, unprocessed foods and eliminates grains, legumes, refined sugars, and processed foods. If you're embarking on a Paleo lifestyle, it's essential to stock your pantry with the right staples and ingredients. Let's explore the foods to eat, avoid, and eat in moderation on a Paleo diet.

Foods to Eat

Fresh Meat and Poultry: Grass-fed beef, pasture-raised poultry, and wild-caught fish are excellent sources of protein and healthy fats. These should form the basis of your Paleo diet.

Eggs: Eggs are a nutrient-dense food and provide high-quality protein. Opt for organic, free-range eggs whenever possible.

Fresh Fruits and Vegetables: Load up on a variety of colorful fruits and vegetables, as they provide essential vitamins, minerals, and antioxidants. Choose organic options when available.

Nuts and Seeds: Almonds, walnuts, cashews, chia seeds, and flaxseeds are Paleo-friendly sources of healthy fats, fiber, and micronutrients.

Healthy Fats and Oils: Avocado oil, olive oil, coconut oil, and ghee (clarified butter) are great choices for cooking and dressing your meals.

Herbs and Spices: Enhance the flavor of your dishes with herbs and spices like basil, oregano, cinnamon, turmeric, and ginger. They add flavor and offer other potential health benefits.

Coconut Products: Coconut milk, coconut flour, and coconut aminos are versatile ingredients that add flavor and texture to Paleo recipes.

Foods to Avoid

Grains and Legumes: Wheat, rice, corn, oats, and legumes like beans, lentils, and peanuts are not part of the Paleo diet due to their high carbohydrate and anti-nutrient content.

Processed Foods: Avoid processed foods such as chips, cookies, sugary cereals, and packaged snacks, as they often contain additives, preservatives, and unhealthy oils.

Dairy Products: Dairy is not considered Paleo-friendly due to lactose intolerance and potential inflammatory effects. However, some individuals choose to include limited amounts of high-quality dairy products like grass-fed butter or ghee.

Refined Sugars: Say goodbye to white sugar, corn syrup, and artificial sweeteners. Instead, opt for natural sweeteners like honey, maple syrup, or dates in moderation.

Foods to Eat in Moderation

Tubers and Starchy Vegetables: While not strictly prohibited, starchy vegetables like sweet potatoes and yams should be eaten in moderation, especially if you're aiming for weight loss.

Fruit: Although fruits are packed with nutrients, they also contain natural sugars. Enjoy them in moderation and focus on lower-sugar options like berries.

Alcohol: Alcohol is not a part of the strict Paleo diet, but if you choose to indulge occasionally, opt for gluten-free spirits or dry wines without added sugars.

Building a well-stocked Paleo pantry will set you up for success on your dietary journey. Below are some pantry staples to consider:

Almond Flour and Coconut Flour: These grain-free flours are excellent alternatives for baking and breading.

Coconut Aminos: A soy sauce substitute that adds flavor to stir-fries and marinades without the gluten and soy.

Nut Butter: Look for varieties made from pure nuts without added sugars or oils.

Canned Fish: Sardines, salmon, and tuna packed in water or olive oil provide convenient sources of omega-3 fatty acids.

Apple Cider Vinegar: This vinegar is a versatile ingredient for dressings, marinades, and various recipes.

Dark Chocolate: Opt for dark chocolate with at least 70% cocoa content for an occasional indulgence.

Remember, everyone's dietary needs and tolerances may vary, so it's important to listen to your body and make adjustments accordingly. Building a Paleo pantry and following the principles of the diet will help you achieve better health, increased energy, and improved overall well-being.

As usual, before making any significant dietary changes, it is advisable to speak with a medical practitioner or qualified nutritionist. They can provide personalized guidance and support to ensure that the Paleo diet is suitable for your individual needs.

CHAPTER THREE

Breakfast Delights: Energizing Paleo Air Fryer Recipes

Crispy Bacon and Egg Cups:

Ingredients:
- 6 slices of nitrate-free bacon
- 6 large eggs
- Salt and pepper to taste
- Chopped fresh herbs (optional, for garnish)

Instructions:
- Preheat your air fryer to 350°F (175°C).
- Line each cavity of a muffin tin with a slice of bacon, creating a cup shape.
- Crack an egg into each bacon cup.
- Season with salt and pepper.

- Place the muffin tin in the air fryer basket and cook for 10-12 minutes, or until the bacon is crispy and the eggs are cooked to your desired doneness.
- Garnish with chopped fresh herbs if desired. Serve warm.

Sweet Potato Hash Browns

Ingredients:
- 2 medium sweet potatoes, grated
- 1 small onion, finely chopped
- 1 tablespoon coconut flour
- 1 teaspoon paprika
- Salt and pepper to taste
- Coconut oil, for greasing

Instructions:
- In a bowl, combine the grated sweet potatoes, chopped onion, coconut flour, paprika, salt, and pepper.
- Mix well until everything is evenly combined.

- Grease the air fryer basket with coconut oil.
- Form small patties with the sweet potato mixture and place them in the air fryer basket.
- Cook at 400°F (200°C) for 12-15 minutes, flipping halfway through, until the hash browns are golden brown and crispy.
- Serve hot as a side dish or breakfast option.

Veggie Omelette

Ingredients:
- 3 large eggs
- 1/4 cup chopped bell peppers
- 1/4 cup chopped mushrooms
- 1/4 cup chopped spinach
- Salt and pepper to taste
- Cooking spray or olive oil for greasing

Instructions:
- Whisk the eggs in a bowl until well beaten.

- Add the chopped bell peppers, mushrooms, and spinach to the eggs. Season with salt and pepper.
- Grease a small oven-safe dish or ramekin with cooking spray or olive oil.
- Pour the egg mixture into the greased dish.
- Place the dish in the air fryer basket and cook at 350°F (175°C) for 8-10 minutes, or until the eggs are set and cooked through.
- Carefully remove the dish from the air fryer and let it cool slightly before serving.

Banana Walnut Muffins

Ingredients:
- 2 ripe bananas, mashed
- 2 large eggs
- 1/4 cup almond flour
- 1/4 cup coconut flour
- 1/4 cup chopped walnuts
- 1 tablespoon honey (optional)

- 1 teaspoon baking powder
- 1/2 teaspoon cinnamon
- Pinch of salt

Instructions:

- Mix together the mashed bananas and eggs in a bowl until well combined.
- Add the almond flour, coconut flour, chopped walnuts, honey (if desired), baking powder, cinnamon, and salt. Stir until all ingredients are incorporated.
- Preheat your air fryer to 325°F (160°C).
- Divide the batter evenly among silicone muffin cups or a greased muffin tin.
- Place the muffin cups or tin in the air fryer basket and cook for 15-18 minutes, or until a toothpick inserted into the center of a muffin comes out clean.
- Allow the muffins to cool before removing them from the cups or tin. Enjoy as a grab-and-go breakfast option.

Cinnamon Apple Chips

Ingredients:

- 2 apples, thinly sliced
- 1 teaspoon ground cinnamon
- Optional: 1 teaspoon coconut sugar or sweetener of choice

Instructions:

- Preheat your air fryer to 350°F (175°C).
- In a bowl, toss the apple slices with cinnamon and optional sweetener until evenly coated.
- The coated apple slices should be placed in a single layer in the air fryer basket.
- Cook for ten to twelve minutes, flipping the slices halfway through, until they are crispy and slightly golden.
- Remove them from the air fryer and let them cool completely before serving. As they cool, they become crispier.

CHAPTER FOUR

Appetizers and Snacks: Crispy Bites of Paleo Perfection

Crispy Sweet Potato Fries

Ingredients:

- 2 large sweet potatoes, cut into fries
- 1 tablespoon avocado oil
- 1 teaspoon paprika
- 1/2 teaspoon garlic powder
- Salt and pepper to taste

Instructions:

- Preheat your air fryer to 400°F (200°C).
- In a bowl, toss the sweet potato fries with avocado oil, paprika, garlic powder, salt, and pepper until well coated.
- Place the seasoned sweet potato fries in the air fryer basket in a single layer.

- Cook for 15-18 minutes, flipping the fries halfway through, until they are golden brown and crispy.
- Remove them from the air fryer and let them cool slightly before serving. Enjoy with your favorite dipping sauce.

Crispy Chicken Wings

Ingredients:
- 1 pound chicken wings
- 1 tablespoon coconut oil or ghee
- 1 teaspoon paprika
- 1/2 teaspoon garlic powder
- 1/2 teaspoon onion powder
- Salt and pepper to taste

Instructions:
- Preheat your air fryer to 400°F (200°C).
- In a bowl, toss the chicken wings with coconut oil or ghee, paprika, garlic powder, onion powder, salt, and pepper until well coated.

- Place the seasoned chicken wings in the air fryer basket in a single layer.
- Cook for 20-25 minutes, flipping the wings halfway through, until they are crispy and cooked through.
- Remove them from the air fryer. Let them cool for a few minutes before serving. Enjoy with your favorite dipping sauce.

Zucchini Fritters

Ingredients:

- 2 medium zucchinis, grated
- 1/4 cup almond flour
- 1/4 cup coconut flour
- 2 green onions, finely chopped
- 2 large eggs, beaten
- 1 teaspoon dried basil
- Salt and pepper to taste
- Avocado oil or cooking spray

Instructions:

- In a bowl, combine the grated zucchini, almond flour, coconut flour, green onions, beaten eggs, dried basil, salt, and pepper. Mix everything thoroughly until it is all combined.
- Preheat your air fryer to 375°F (190°C).
- Grease the air fryer basket with avocado oil or cooking spray.
- Form small patties with the zucchini mixture and place them in the air fryer basket.
- Cook the fritters for 12 to 15 minutes, flipping them halfway through, or until they are crispy and golden brown.
- Remove from the air fryer. Let them cool slightly before serving. Enjoy as a snack or appetizer.

Stuffed Mushrooms

Ingredients:
- 12 large button mushrooms
- 1/2 pound ground sausage (Paleo-friendly)
- 1/4 cup almond flour

- 2 green onions, finely chopped
- 2 tablespoons nutritional yeast (optional)
- Salt and pepper to taste

Instructions:

- The mushroom stems should be removed and kept aside.
- In a skillet, cook the ground sausage over medium heat until browned. Drain any excess fat.
- In a bowl, combine the cooked sausage, almond flour, green onions, nutritional yeast (if using), salt, and pepper. Mix well.
- Use the sausage mixture to fill each mushroom cap.
- Preheat your air fryer to 375°F (190°C).
- Put the stuffed mushrooms in a single layer in the air fryer basket.
- Cook for 12-15 minutes until the mushrooms are tender and the filling is golden brown.
- Before serving, take them out of the air fryer and let them cool for a while. Enjoy as a tasty appetizer.

Coconut Shrimp

Ingredients:

- 1 pound large shrimp, peeled and deveined
- 1/2 cup almond flour
- 1/2 cup unsweetened shredded coconut
- 2 large eggs, beaten
- Salt and pepper to taste

Instructions:

- Preheat your air fryer to 400°F (200°C).
- In one bowl, place the almond flour. In another bowl, place the beaten eggs. Salt and pepper should be added to the shredded coconut in a third bowl.
- Dip each shrimp into the almond flour, then the beaten eggs, and finally coat it with the shredded coconut mixture.
- Place the coated shrimp in the air fryer basket in a single layer.

- Cook for 8 to 10 minutes, flipping the shrimp halfway through, until they are crispy and golden brown.
- Remove them from the air fryer. Let them cool slightly before serving. Enjoy with a dipping sauce of your choice.

CHAPTER FIVE

Wholesome Chicken and Poultry Dishes: A Flavorful Twist

Crispy Air Fryer Chicken Tenders

Ingredients:

- 1 pound chicken tenders
- 1/2 cup almond flour
- 1 teaspoon paprika
- 1/2 teaspoon garlic powder
- 1/2 teaspoon onion powder
- Salt and pepper to taste
- 2 large eggs, beaten

Instructions:

- Preheat your air fryer to 400°F (200°C).

- In a bowl, combine the almond flour, paprika, garlic powder, onion powder, salt, and pepper.
- Dip each chicken tender into the beaten eggs, then coat it with the almond flour mixture, pressing to adhere.
- The coated chicken tenders should be placed in the air fryer basket in a single layer.
- Cook for 10-12 minutes, flipping the tenders halfway through, until they are golden brown and cooked through.
- Before serving, take them out of the air fryer and let them cool for a while. Enjoy with your favorite dipping sauce.

Lemon Herb Air Fryer Chicken Breast

Ingredients:
- 2 boneless, skinless chicken breasts
- 2 tablespoons olive oil
- 1 tablespoon fresh lemon juice
- 1 teaspoon dried thyme

- 1 teaspoon dried rosemary
- 1/2 teaspoon garlic powder
- Salt and pepper to taste

Instructions:

- Preheat your air fryer to 375°F (190°C).
- In a small bowl, mix together the olive oil, lemon juice, dried thyme, dried rosemary, garlic powder, salt, and pepper.
- Rub the chicken breasts with the prepared mixture, making sure to coat them evenly.
- The chicken breasts should be placed in the air fryer basket.
- Cook for 18-20 minutes, flipping the chicken halfway through, until they are cooked through and reach an internal temperature of 165°F (74°C).
- After removing them from the air fryer, give them some time to settle before slicing. Serve with your favorite side dishes.

Buffalo Air Fryer Wings

Ingredients:

- 2 pounds chicken wings
- 2 tablespoons ghee or coconut oil, melted
- 1/4 cup hot sauce (check for Paleo-friendly options)
- 1 teaspoon garlic powder
- 1/2 teaspoon paprika
- Salt and pepper to taste

Instructions:

- Preheat your air fryer to 400°F (200°C).
- In a bowl, combine the melted ghee or coconut oil, hot sauce, garlic powder, paprika, salt, and pepper.
- Chicken wings should be fully coated after being tossed in the prepared sauce.
- Put the coated chicken wings in a single layer in the air fryer basket.
- Cook for 20-25 minutes, flipping the wings halfway through, until they are crispy and cooked through.

- Remove from the air fryer. Allow them to cool for a few minutes before serving. Enjoy with celery sticks and a side of Paleo ranch dressing.

Herb-Roasted Air Fryer Turkey Breast

Ingredients:
- 2 pounds turkey breast, boneless and skinless
- 2 tablespoons olive oil
- 1 teaspoon dried sage
- 1 teaspoon dried thyme
- 1 teaspoon dried rosemary
- 1/2 teaspoon garlic powder
- Salt and pepper to taste

Instructions:
- Preheat your air fryer to 375°F (190°C).
- In a small bowl, mix together the olive oil, dried sage, dried thyme, dried rosemary, garlic powder, salt, and pepper.

- Rub the turkey breast with the prepared mixture, making sure to coat it evenly.
- The turkey breast should be placed in the air fryer basket.
- Cook for 30-35 minutes, flipping the turkey halfway through, until it reaches an internal temperature of 165°F (74°C).
- Remove from the air fryer and let it rest for a few minutes before slicing. Serve with your favorite vegetables.

Moroccan Spiced Air Fryer Cornish Hens

Ingredients:

- 2 Cornish hens
- 2 tablespoons olive oil
- 1 teaspoon ground cumin
- 1 teaspoon ground coriander
- 1 teaspoon ground paprika
- 1/2 teaspoon ground cinnamon
- Salt and pepper to taste

Instructions:

- Preheat your air fryer to 375°F (190°C).
- In a small bowl, mix together the olive oil, ground cumin, ground coriander, ground paprika, ground cinnamon, salt, and pepper.
- Rub the Cornish hens with the prepared mixture, making sure to coat them evenly.
- Place the Cornish hens in the air fryer basket.
- Cook for 30-35 minutes, flipping the hens halfway through, until they are cooked through and reach an internal temperature of 165°F (74°C).
- Before serving, take them out of the air fryer and allow them to rest for a while. Enjoy with some roasted vegetables on the side.

CHAPTER SIX

Succulent Seafood: Oceanic Delights Made Paleo

Crispy Air Fryer Coconut Shrimp

Ingredients:
- 1 pound shrimp, peeled and deveined
- 1/2 cup almond flour
- 1/2 cup shredded unsweetened coconut
- 1 teaspoon paprika
- 1/2 teaspoon garlic powder
- Salt and pepper to taste
- 2 large eggs, beaten

Instructions:
- Preheat your air fryer to 400°F (200°C).
- In a bowl, combine the almond flour, shredded coconut, paprika, garlic powder, salt, and pepper.

- Dip each shrimp into the beaten eggs, then coat it with the coconut mixture, pressing to adhere.
- Place the coated shrimp in the air fryer basket in a single layer.
- Cook for 8-10 minutes, flipping the shrimp halfway through, until they are golden brown and cooked through.
- After removing them from the air fryer, give them some time to rest before serving.

Lemon Garlic Air Fryer Salmon

Ingredients:

- 2 salmon fillets
- 2 tablespoons olive oil
- 1 tablespoon fresh lemon juice
- 2 cloves garlic, minced
- 1 teaspoon dried dill
- Salt and pepper to taste

Instructions:

- Preheat your air fryer to 400°F (200°C).
- Mix together the minced garlic, olive oil, lemon juice, dried dill, salt, and pepper in a small bowl.
- Brush the salmon fillets with the prepared mixture, making sure to coat them evenly.
- The salmon fillets should be placed in the air fryer basket.
- Cook for 10-12 minutes, or until the salmon flakes easily with a fork.
- Before serving, remove them from the air fryer and give them some time to rest. Serve with a squeeze of fresh lemon juice.

Cajun Air Fryer Shrimp Skewers

Ingredients:

- 1 pound shrimp, peeled and deveined
- 2 tablespoons olive oil
- 1 tablespoon Cajun seasoning
- 1/2 teaspoon paprika

- 1/2 teaspoon garlic powder
- Salt and pepper to taste
- Skewers (wooden skewers should be soaked in water for 30 minutes prior to use).

Instructions:
- Preheat your air fryer to 400°F (200°C).
- In a bowl, combine the olive oil, Cajun seasoning, paprika, garlic powder, salt, and pepper.
- Thread the shrimp onto skewers.
- Brush the shrimp skewers with the prepared mixture, making sure to coat them evenly.
- The shrimp skewers should be placed in the air fryer basket.
- Cook for 6-8 minutes, flipping the skewers halfway through, until the shrimp are cooked through and slightly charred.
- Before serving, remove them from the air fryer and give them some time to rest. Enjoy with a squeeze of fresh lemon juice.

Garlic Butter Air Fryer Scallops

Ingredients:

- 1 pound scallops
- 2 tablespoons ghee or clarified butter, melted
- 2 cloves garlic, minced
- 1 tablespoon fresh parsley, chopped
- Salt and pepper to taste

Instructions:

- Preheat your air fryer to 400°F (200°C).
- In a small bowl, mix together the melted ghee or clarified butter, minced garlic, chopped parsley, salt, and pepper.
- Scallops should be dried with a paper towel.
- Brush the scallops with the prepared mixture, making sure to coat them evenly.
- Place the scallops in the air fryer basket.
- Cook for 6-8 minutes, or until the scallops are opaque and slightly browned.

- They should be removed from the air fryer and let rest for a few minutes before serving. Garnish with additional chopped parsley.

Lemon Herb Air Fryer Halibut

Ingredients:
- 2 halibut fillets
- 2 tablespoons olive oil
- 1 tablespoon fresh lemon juice
- 1 teaspoon dried thyme
- 1/2 teaspoon dried rosemary
- Salt and pepper to taste

Instructions:
- Preheat your air fryer to 400°F (200°C).
- In a small bowl, mix together the olive oil, lemon juice, dried thyme, dried rosemary, salt, and pepper.
- Brush the halibut fillets with the prepared mixture, making sure to coat them evenly.
- Place the halibut fillets in the air fryer basket.

- Halibut should be cooked for 10 to 12 minutes, or until it flakes readily with a fork.
- Before serving, take them out of the air fryer and allow them to rest for a while. Squeeze fresh lemon juice over the halibut before enjoying.

CHAPTER SEVEN

Tender and Juicy Beef, Pork, and Lamb Recipes

Air Fryer Steak Bites

Ingredients:
- 1 pound beef sirloin steak, cut into bite-sized pieces
- 1 tablespoon olive oil
- 1 teaspoon garlic powder
- 1 teaspoon onion powder
- 1/2 teaspoon smoked paprika
- Salt and pepper to taste

Instructions:
- Preheat your air fryer to 400°F (200°C).
- In a bowl, combine the onion powder, smoked paprika, olive oil, garlic powder, salt, and pepper.

- Toss the steak bites in the mixture, ensuring they are evenly coated.
- Place the steak bites in the air fryer basket in a single layer.
- Cook for eight to ten minutes, flipping the steak bites halfway through, until they reach your desired level of doneness.
- Remove them from the air fryer. Let them rest for a few minutes before serving. Enjoy them as a tasty, protein-packed snack or add them to a salad.

Crispy Air Fryer Pork Chops

Ingredients:
- 2 bone-in pork chops
- 1/4 cup almond flour
- 1/4 cup tapioca flour
- 1 teaspoon garlic powder
- 1 teaspoon paprika
- Salt and pepper to taste
- 1 egg, beaten

Instructions:

- Preheat your air fryer to 400°F (200°C).
- In a shallow bowl, mix together the almond flour, tapioca flour, garlic powder, paprika, salt, and pepper.
- Dip each pork chop into the beaten egg, then coat it with the flour mixture, pressing to adhere.
- The pork chops should be placed in the air fryer basket.
- Cook for 12-15 minutes, flipping the pork chops halfway through, until they are crispy and cooked through.
- Remove from the air fryer. Allow them rest for a few minutes before serving. Serve with your favorite side dish or vegetable.

Garlic Herb Air Fryer Lamb Chops

Ingredients:

- 4 lamb chops
- 2 tablespoons olive oil
- 2 cloves garlic, minced
- 1 teaspoon dried rosemary
- 1 teaspoon dried thyme
- Salt and pepper to taste

Instructions:
- Preheat your air fryer to 400°F (200°C).
- Combine the olive oil, minced garlic, dried thyme, dried rosemary, salt, and pepper in a small bowl.
- Brush both sides of the lamb chops with the prepared mixture.
- The lamb chops should be placed in the air fryer basket.
- Cook for 10-12 minutes, flipping the lamb chops halfway through, until they reach your desired level of doneness.
- Remove from the air fryer. Let them rest for a few minutes before serving. Serve with a side of roasted vegetables.

Spicy Air Fryer Meatballs

Ingredients:

- 1 pound ground beef
- 1/4 cup almond flour
- 1/4 cup finely chopped onion
- 2 cloves garlic, minced
- 1 tablespoon chopped fresh parsley
- 1 teaspoon dried oregano
- 1/2 teaspoon chili powder
- Salt and pepper to taste

Instructions:

- Preheat your air fryer to 400°F (200°C).
- In a bowl, combine the ground beef, almond flour, chopped onion, minced garlic, chopped parsley, dried oregano, chili powder, salt, and pepper. Mix until well combined.
- Make meatballs out of the mixture that are about an inch in diameter.

- The meatballs should be arranged in a single layer in the air fryer basket.
- Cook for 10-12 minutes, shaking the basket halfway through, until the meatballs are cooked through.
- Before serving, take them out of the air fryer and let them cool. Serve with your favorite dipping sauce or as a topping for zucchini noodles.

Smoky Air Fryer Ribs

Ingredients:
- 1 rack of pork ribs
- 2 tablespoons smoked paprika
- 1 tablespoon garlic powder
- 1 tablespoon onion powder
- 1 teaspoon cayenne pepper
- Salt and pepper to taste
- BBQ sauce (optional)

Instructions:
- Preheat your air fryer to 360°F (180°C).

- In a small bowl, mix together the smoked paprika, garlic powder, onion powder, cayenne pepper, salt, and pepper.
- Rub the spice mixture all over the rack of ribs, ensuring it is evenly coated.
- The ribs should be placed in the air fryer basket, meat-side down.
- Cook for 30 minutes, then flip the ribs and cook for an additional 30 minutes.
- If desired, brush the ribs with BBQ sauce during the last 5 minutes of cooking.

CHAPTER EIGHT

Flavorful Vegetable Creations: A Plant-Powered Feast

Crispy Air Fryer Brussels Sprouts

Ingredients:
- 1 pound Brussels sprouts, trimmed and halved
- 2 tablespoons olive oil
- 1 teaspoon garlic powder
- 1/2 teaspoon smoked paprika
- Salt and pepper to taste

Instructions:
- Preheat your air fryer to 400°F (200°C).
- In a bowl, toss the Brussels sprouts with olive oil, garlic powder, smoked paprika, salt, and pepper until they are evenly coated.

- The Brussels sprouts should be placed in the air fryer basket in a single layer.
- It should be cooked for 12-15 minutes, shaking the basket halfway through, until they are crispy and golden brown.
- Remove from the air fryer and serve immediately. Enjoy as a tasty snack or side dish.

Parmesan Air Fryer Asparagus

Ingredients:
- 1 bunch asparagus, trimmed
- 2 tablespoons olive oil
- 1/4 cup grated Parmesan cheese
- 1 teaspoon garlic powder
- Salt and pepper to taste

Instructions:
- Preheat your air fryer to 400°F (200°C).

- In a bowl, toss the asparagus with olive oil, Parmesan cheese, garlic powder, salt, and pepper until they are well coated.
- Asparagus should be placed in a single layer in the air fryer basket.
- Cook for 8-10 minutes, shaking the basket halfway through, until the asparagus is tender and the cheese is melted and golden.
- Remove from the air fryer and serve immediately. Enjoy it as a nutritious and delicious side dish.

Spicy Air Fryer Cauliflower Bites

Ingredients:

- 1 head cauliflower, cut into florets
- 2 tablespoons olive oil
- 1 teaspoon paprika
- 1/2 teaspoon chili powder
- 1/2 teaspoon cumin
- Salt and pepper to taste

Instructions:

- Preheat your air fryer to 400°F (200°C).
- In a bowl, toss the cauliflower florets with olive oil, paprika, chili powder, cumin, salt, and pepper until they are evenly coated.
- The cauliflower should be placed in the air fryer basket in a single layer.
- Cook for 15-18 minutes, shaking the basket halfway through, until the cauliflower is tender and crispy.
- Remove from the air fryer and serve immediately. Enjoy as a spicy and flavorful appetizer.

Herb-Roasted Air Fryer Carrots

Ingredients:

- 1 pound peeled carrots, cut into sticks
- 2 tablespoons olive oil
- 1 teaspoon dried thyme
- 1 teaspoon dried rosemary
- Salt and pepper to taste

Instructions:

- Preheat your air fryer to 400°F (200°C).
- In a bowl, toss the carrot sticks with olive oil, dried thyme, dried rosemary, salt, and pepper until they are well coated.
- The carrots should be placed in the air fryer basket in a single layer.
- Cook for 12-15 minutes, shaking the basket halfway through, until the carrots are tender and lightly browned.
- Remove from the air fryer and serve immediately. Enjoy as a flavorful side dish.

Crispy Air Fryer Zucchini Fries

Ingredients:

- 2 zucchinis, cut into sticks
- 1/2 cup almond flour
- 1/4 cup grated Parmesan cheese
- 1 teaspoon garlic powder
- 1 teaspoon paprika

- Salt and pepper to taste
- 2 eggs, beaten

Instructions:

- Preheat your air fryer to 400°F (200°C).
- In a shallow bowl, mix together almond flour, garlic powder, paprika, salt, grated Parmesan cheese, and pepper.
- Dip each zucchini stick into the beaten eggs, then coat it with the almond flour mixture.
- Place the coated zucchini sticks in the air fryer basket in a single layer.
- Cook for 10-12 minutes, shaking the basket halfway through, until the zucchini fries are crispy and golden.
- Remove from the air fryer and serve immediately. It should be enjoyed as a tasty and healthy snack.

CHAPTER NINE

Side Dishes and Sauces: Perfect Complements to Any Meal

Garlic Rosemary Air Fryer Sweet Potato Wedges

Ingredients:
- 2 medium sweet potatoes, cut into wedges
- 2 tablespoons olive oil
- 2 cloves garlic, minced
- 1 tablespoon chopped fresh rosemary
- Salt and pepper to taste

Instructions:
- Preheat your air fryer to 400°F (200°C).
- Sweet potato wedges should be thoroughly coated in a bowl with olive oil, minced garlic, chopped rosemary, salt, and pepper.

- The sweet potato wedges should be placed in the air fryer basket in a single layer.
- Cook for 15-20 minutes, shaking the basket halfway through, until the sweet potatoes are tender and lightly browned.
- Remove from the air fryer and serve immediately. Enjoy as a flavorful and healthy side dish.

Crispy Air Fryer Onion Rings

Ingredients:
- 1 large onion, sliced into rings
- 1/2 cup almond flour
- 1/4 cup arrowroot flour
- 1 teaspoon garlic powder
- 1/2 teaspoon paprika
- Salt and pepper to taste
- 2 eggs, beaten

Instructions:
- Preheat your air fryer to 400°F (200°C).

- In a shallow bowl, mix together almond flour, paprika, salt, arrowroot flour, garlic powder, and pepper.
- Dip each onion ring into the beaten eggs, then coat it with the flour mixture.
- Place the coated onion rings in the air fryer basket in a single layer.
- Cook for 10-12 minutes, shaking the basket halfway through, until the onion rings are crispy and golden.
- Remove from the air fryer and serve immediately. Enjoy as a delicious and guilt-free snack or side dish.

Lemon Garlic Air Fryer Broccoli

Ingredients:

- 1 head broccoli, cut into florets
- 2 tablespoons olive oil
- 2 cloves garlic, minced
- Juice of 1 lemon

- Salt and pepper to taste

Instructions:
- Preheat your air fryer to 375°F (190°C).
- In a bowl, toss the broccoli florets with olive oil, minced garlic, lemon juice, salt, and pepper until they are well coated.
- Place the broccoli florets in the air fryer basket in a single layer.
- Cook for 8-10 minutes, shaking the basket halfway through, until the broccoli is tender and lightly charred.
- Remove from the air fryer and serve immediately. Squeeze some fresh lemon juice over the top if desired. Enjoy as a zesty and nutritious side dish.

Creamy Avocado Dip

Ingredients:
- 2 ripe avocados
- Juice of 1 lime

- 1 clove garlic, minced
- 2 tablespoons chopped fresh cilantro
- Salt and pepper to taste

Instructions:

- Mash the avocados in a bowl until smooth.
- Stir in lime juice, minced garlic, chopped cilantro, salt, and pepper.
- Place the avocado dip in a serving bowl and refrigerate for at least 30 minutes to allow the flavors to blend.
- Serve with sliced vegetables, sweet potato fries, or as a topping for grilled meats. Enjoy the creamy and flavorful dip.

Tangy Balsamic Glaze

Ingredients:

- 1/2 cup balsamic vinegar
- 2 tablespoons honey
- 1/2 teaspoon Dijon mustard

Instructions:

- In a small saucepan, whisk together balsamic vinegar, honey, and Dijon mustard.
- The mixture should be brought to a boil over medium heat. Then reduce the heat to low.
- Simmer for about 10 minutes, stirring occasionally, until the glaze has thickened and coats the back of a spoon.
- Remove from heat and let it cool slightly before using.
- Drizzle the tangy balsamic glaze over grilled vegetables, roasted meats, or use it as a dipping sauce. Enjoy the sweet and savory flavors.

CHAPTER TEN

Irresistible Paleo Air Fryer Desserts: Satisfy Your Sweet Tooth

Coconut Flour Chocolate Chip Cookies

Ingredients:
- 1/2 cup coconut flour
- 1/4 cup coconut oil, melted
- 1/4 cup maple syrup
- 2 eggs
- 1 teaspoon vanilla extract
- 1/4 teaspoon baking soda
- Pinch of sea salt
- 1/2 cup dairy-free dark chocolate chips

Instructions:
- Preheat your air fryer to 350°F (175°C).

- In a bowl, mix together coconut flour, melted coconut oil, maple syrup, eggs, vanilla extract, baking soda, and sea salt until well combined.
- Fold in the dark chocolate chips.
- Scoop the dough onto a baking sheet that has been covered with parchment paper in tablespoon-sized chunks.
- Place the cookies in the air fryer basket in a single layer (you may need to cook them in batches).
- Cook for 8-10 minutes, until they are golden and firm.
- Remove from the air fryer and let them cool before serving. Enjoy these chewy and chocolatey cookies guilt-free.

Apple Crisp

Ingredients:

- 4 apples, peeled, cored, and sliced
- 1 tablespoon coconut oil, melted
- 1 tablespoon maple syrup

- 1/2 cup almond flour
- 1/4 cup coconut flour
- 1/4 cup shredded coconut
- 1/4 cup chopped pecans
- 2 tablespoons coconut sugar
- 1 teaspoon ground cinnamon
- Pinch of sea salt

Instructions:

- Preheat your air fryer to 375°F (190°C).
- In a bowl, mix together melted coconut oil and maple syrup.
- Toss the sliced apples in the coconut oil and maple syrup mixture until well coated.
- In a separate bowl, combine almond flour, coconut flour, shredded coconut, chopped pecans, coconut sugar, ground cinnamon, and sea salt.
- Place the coated apples in the air fryer basket and sprinkle the crumb topping evenly over the apples.
- Cook for 10-12 minutes, until the apples are tender and the topping is golden and crisp.

- Remove from the air fryer and let it cool slightly before serving. Enjoy this warm and comforting apple crisp.

Paleo Donuts

Ingredients:
- 2 cups almond flour
- 1/4 cup coconut flour
- 1/4 cup tapioca flour
- 1/4 cup coconut sugar
- 1 teaspoon baking powder
- 1/4 teaspoon sea salt
- 1/2 cup almond milk
- 1/4 cup coconut oil, melted
- 2 eggs
- 1 teaspoon vanilla extract
- Paleo-friendly chocolate glaze or powdered sugar for topping (optional)

Instructions:

- Preheat your air fryer to 350°F (175°C).
- In a bowl, whisk together almond flour, coconut flour, tapioca flour, coconut sugar, baking powder, and sea salt.
- In a separate bowl, whisk together almond milk, melted coconut oil, eggs, and vanilla extract.
- Pour the wet ingredients into the dry ingredients and mix until a smooth batter forms.
- Grease the cavities of a donut pan with coconut oil or use silicone donut molds.
- Spoon the batter into the donut cavities, filling them about three-quarters full.
- Place the donut pan in the air fryer basket and cook for 8-10 minutes, until the donuts are golden and firm.
- Remove from the air fryer and let them cool before adding the desired topping. Enjoy these delicious and healthier Paleo donuts.

Cinnamon-Spiced Sweet Potato Fries

Ingredients:

- 2 large sweet potatoes, cut into fries
- 2 tablespoons avocado oil
- 1 tablespoon coconut sugar
- 1 teaspoon ground cinnamon
- Pinch of sea salt

Instructions:

- Preheat your air fryer to 400°F (200°C).
- In a bowl, toss the sweet potato fries with avocado oil until well coated.
- In a separate bowl, combine coconut sugar, ground cinnamon, and sea salt.
- Sprinkle the cinnamon-sugar mixture over the sweet potato fries and toss to coat evenly.
- Place the seasoned sweet potato fries in the air fryer basket in a single layer.

- Cook for 15-18 minutes, shaking the basket halfway through, until the fries are crispy and golden.
- Remove from the air fryer. Let them cool slightly before serving. Enjoy these flavorful and guilt-free sweet potato fries.

Coconut Shrimp

Ingredients:
- 1 pound shrimp, peeled and deveined
- 1/2 cup almond flour
- 1/4 cup shredded coconut
- 1 teaspoon paprika
- 1/2 teaspoon garlic powder
- 1/4 teaspoon sea salt
- 2 eggs, beaten
- Paleo-friendly dipping sauce of your choice (optional)

Instructions:
- Preheat your air fryer to 400°F (200°C).

- In a bowl, combine almond flour, shredded coconut, paprika, garlic powder, and sea salt.
- Dip each shrimp into the beaten eggs, then coat it in the almond flour and coconut mixture.
- The coated shrimp should be placed in the air fryer basket in a single layer.
- Cook for 8-10 minutes, flipping them halfway through, until the shrimp are crispy and cooked through.
- It should be removed from the air fryer. Also, let them cool slightly before serving. Serve with your favorite paleo-friendly dipping sauce, if desired. Enjoy these crunchy and flavorful coconut shrimp.

CHAPTER ELEVEN

Tips and Tricks for Perfect Paleo Air Frying

Unlocking the full potential of your air fryer for Paleo cooking can be a game-changer when it comes to preparing delicious and healthy meals. With the right tips and tricks, you can achieve perfectly crispy and flavorful Paleo dishes that satisfy your cravings and nourish your body. In this guide, we'll explore the key tips and tricks for perfect Paleo air frying. Get ready to elevate your air fryer cooking skills and create culinary masterpieces that adhere to your Paleo lifestyle.

Preheating: Just like with traditional cooking methods, preheating your air fryer is crucial. This allows the air fryer to reach the optimal temperature before you start cooking. Preheating is necessary to ensure even cooking and crispy results. Follow the manufacturer's instructions for preheating time and temperature, usually around 3-5 minutes at the desired cooking temperature.

Use the Right Cooking Oil: When air frying, it's important to choose the right cooking oil. Paleo-friendly oils like avocado oil, coconut oil, or olive oil are excellent choices. These oils have high smoke points and add delicious flavor to your dishes. Lightly coat your ingredients with oil before placing them in the air fryer for better browning and texture.

Don't Overcrowd the Basket: To achieve crispy and evenly cooked results, avoid overcrowding the air fryer basket. Leave enough space between the ingredients to allow hot air to circulate freely. If you have a large batch to cook, it's better to cook in multiple batches for optimal results.

Shake and Flip: Shake or flip your ingredients halfway through the cooking process to ensure even browning and crispness. This helps to promote even cooking and prevents any areas from becoming too dark. Use tongs or a spatula to gently turn or shake the ingredients, being careful not to damage the coating or breading.

Adjust Cooking Time and Temperature: Different air fryer models may vary in terms of cooking time and temperature. It's important to experiment and adjust the settings based on your specific air fryer and desired results. Start with the recommended cooking time and temperature in recipes, and then make adjustments as needed to achieve your preferred level of crispness.

Use Parchment Paper or Silicone Liners: To prevent ingredients from sticking to the air fryer basket, consider using parchment paper or silicone liners. These non-stick surfaces create a barrier between the food and the basket, making it easier to remove the cooked items without any sticking issues. Just make sure the parchment paper or silicone liner is compatible with your air fryer model.

Keep an Eye on Cooking Progress: Air frying can be quick, and the cooking time may vary depending on the recipe and ingredient size. It's essential to keep an eye on the cooking progress to avoid overcooking or under-cooking. Open the air fryer occasionally to check the color and texture of the food. To get the required level of doneness, adjust the cooking time accordingly.

Season and Spice Up: Enhance the flavors of your Paleo air-fried dishes by using a variety of herbs, spices, and seasonings. Experiment with different combinations to create unique and tasty flavors. From garlic powder and paprika to cumin and turmeric, the options are endless. Don't be afraid to get creative and add a burst of flavor to your dishes.

Clean and Maintain: Proper cleaning and maintenance of your air fryer are essential for optimal performance. Always refer to the manufacturer's instructions for cleaning guidelines. Most air fryers have removable parts that are dishwasher safe, making the cleanup process easy. Regularly clean the air fryer basket, tray, and exterior to remove any residue or grease buildup.

Experiment and Have Fun: The beauty of Paleo air frying is the opportunity to experiment with a wide range of ingredients and recipes. Don't be afraid to try new flavors, ingredients, and techniques. Have fun in the kitchen and let your creative side shine. You might discover some incredible flavor combinations and create your own signature Paleo air fryer recipes.

With these tips and tricks, you're well on your way to mastering the art of Paleo air frying. Enjoy the convenience, flavor, and health benefits of air-fried Paleo meals that are sure to impress your taste buds and support your Paleo lifestyle. Get ready to savor crispy, delicious dishes while nourishing your body with wholesome, nutrient-dense ingredients.

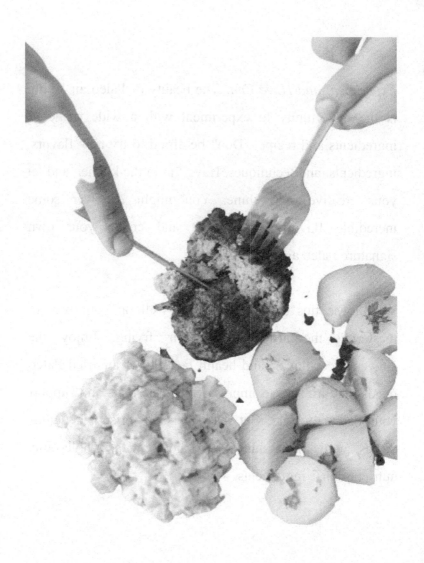

CONCLUSION

In conclusion, the Paleo Air Fryer Cookbook opens up a world of culinary possibilities that not only satisfy your cravings but also nourish your body with wholesome, nutrient-dense ingredients. By harnessing the power of the air fryer and embracing the principles of the Paleo diet, you can enjoy a wide variety of delicious, crispy, and healthy dishes that are both satisfying and good for you.

One of the key aspects of the Paleo lifestyle is the focus on real, whole foods. This cookbook takes that principle and combines it with the convenience and versatility of the air fryer to create a collection of recipes that are not only delicious but also align with your dietary goals. From crispy chicken tenders to flavorful vegetable medleys, each recipe is thoughtfully crafted to provide you with a satisfying and wholesome meal.

One of the most remarkable things about the Paleo diet is its ability to satisfy your cravings in a healthier way. By eliminating processed foods, grains, and refined sugars, the Paleo diet encourages you to explore the rich flavors and textures of natural ingredients. The recipes in this cookbook showcase the incredible variety and versatility of the Paleo diet, proving that you don't have to sacrifice taste to eat healthily.

Furthermore, the air fryer becomes your ally in creating these delectable dishes. Its innovative cooking technology allows you to achieve that desired crispy texture without the need for excessive oil or frying. It's a healthier alternative to traditional frying methods, reducing the amount of unhealthy fats while still delivering that satisfying crunch.

By following the recipes in this cookbook, you can indulge in your favorite comfort foods, such as crispy chicken wings, sweet potato fries, or even decadent desserts, all while staying true to your Paleo lifestyle. The use of wholesome ingredients like lean proteins, fresh vegetables, and natural fats ensures that every bite is packed with nutrients and supports your overall well-being.

In addition to the delicious recipes, this cookbook also offers valuable tips and tricks for perfecting your air frying techniques. From preheating the air fryer to flipping the ingredients halfway through cooking, these insights help you achieve optimal results and ensure that every dish is cooked to perfection.

The Paleo Air Fryer Cookbook is not just a collection of recipes; it's a guide to a healthier way of cooking and eating. It empowers you to take control of your health and make mindful choices that will nourish your body. By embracing the Paleo lifestyle and incorporating the air fryer into your cooking routine, you can enjoy meals that are both satisfying and beneficial for your overall well-being.

So, whether you're new to the Paleo diet or a seasoned enthusiast, this cookbook is your go-to resource for creating delicious, nutrient-packed meals using your air fryer. It's a journey of culinary exploration and self-discovery, where you can indulge in your favorite flavors while knowing that you're nourishing your body with wholesome, natural ingredients.

Embrace the power of the air fryer, harness the flavors of the Paleo diet, and let this cookbook be your guide to satisfying your cravings in a healthy and delicious way. It will be beneficial to both your body and taste buds. Get ready to embark on a culinary adventure and experience the joy of Paleo air frying. **Happy cooking!**

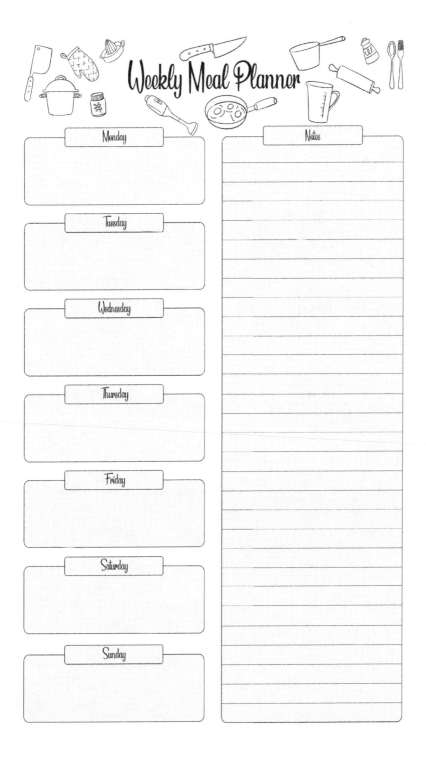

Weekly Meal Planner

Monday

Tuesday

Wednesday

Thursday

Friday

Saturday

Sunday

Notes

Weekly Meal Planner

Monday

Tuesday

Wednesday

Thursday

Friday

Saturday

Sunday

Notes

Weekly Meal Planner

Monday

Tuesday

Wednesday

Thursday

Friday

Saturday

Sunday

Notes

Weekly Meal Planner

Monday

Tuesday

Wednesday

Thursday

Friday

Saturday

Sunday

Notes

Weekly Meal Planner

Monday

Tuesday

Wednesday

Thursday

Friday

Saturday

Sunday

Notes

Weekly Meal Planner

Monday	Notes
Tuesday	
Wednesday	
Thursday	
Friday	
Saturday	
Sunday	

Weekly Meal Planner

Monday

Tuesday

Wednesday

Thursday

Friday

Saturday

Sunday

Notes

Weekly Meal Planner

Monday

Tuesday

Wednesday

Thursday

Friday

Saturday

Sunday

Notes

Made in the USA
Monee, IL
14 April 2024